Positive

Vibes

- KIDS -

YOUR DAILY DOSE OF POSITIVITY!

PRESTON MITCHUM JR.

Positive Vibes Kids

ISBN: 978-1-956581-45-4

Canyon Lake, Texas
www.ErinGoBraghPublishing.com

Introduction

No matter what, author Preston always finds that positive perspective in life. He celebrates the good times and looks for ways to learn through the tough ones. In this very special children's book, his message remains:

POSITIVE THOUGHTS, POSITIVE VIBES.

Riding the wave of his continued success in presenting positivity to adults, Preston felt inspiration to put pen to paper once again, in hopes of bringing some of that wonderful positivity to children's lives as well.

With a little assistance from fellow children's book author, Kathleen J. Shields, Preston presents this wonderful book of inspirational affirmations to enlighten today's youth and help bring positivity to the world. What is your superpower? Positivity!

What are Positive Vibes?

A vibe is energy. It is a feeling. An emotional reaction to goodness and happiness. A good vibe will help your mind and body relax. It is a way of thinking and interacting with the world.

Positive Vibes can be felt and they can be shared. You can show someone positive vibes through your kindness, support, appreciation and even good wishes for them.

One of the simplest ways to share positive vibes is through a smile. If you smile at someone, you show them they matter and that someone cares about them. That feeling will fill a void they did not realize was there. You may not ever know how much that little smile meant to that person, but its impact is greater than you could possibly imagine!

Positive Vibes can help you fulfill your potential, and attract other positive energies in your life. When you look at your life situations with a positive attitude, you are willing yourself to see good. Good in life. Good in others. Good in the difficult situations. When you help others find that same good, you are helping to spread positive vibes to others.

POSITIVE THOUGHTS, POSITIVE VIBES!

Table of Contents

Your Daily Dose of Positivity

Read at least one page of this book every day.

Take each message to heart. Think about it. Apply it to your life, and see where the power of positivity takes you.

This daily dose of positivity is designed to turn your focus from negative to positive. Your manners, your behaviors and your inspirational acts of kindness will help you grow, one day at a time, until you are the adult that will lead the world to greatness.

POSITIVE THOUGHTS, POSITIVE VIBES!

Start Your Day Right

Wake Up with Gratitude

Wake up every morning grateful for the air you breathe and this wonderful life you have. Appreciate the good things around you. How awesome is it to be surrounded by so much love from your parents, grandparents and friends? Life is not always perfect but, you are happy, healthy and safe. You know what, overall, life is pretty darn good and your future looks bright!

Start the Day Right

Spread your wings and soak in the positivity! By soaring into the day, you will find new ways to move forward. We all have our routines or a specific way to start the day. It's important to take a little time in the morning to balance yourself. If your goal is to give your best, you must be your best.

Find that something that can help you start your day off right. How you start your day can play a major part in how it wraps up.

POSITIVE THOUGHTS, POSITIVE VIBES!

Your Superpower

Healing comes from within. My good friend, Jackie Bieber, says her superpower would be the power to heal. Inside you is a superpower so bright it helps you heal and makes you strong. You grow stronger each day mending and healing in every way.

Your superpower of healing can be very powerful. You likely have not seen its full potential yet. To do that, you must look deep down inside your soul and take care of yourself. Look inside and know that you have the power to heal, and your light is healing others.

Keep Smiling

The smile on your face is like pure joy. I love that song by Denise Williams, "I love your smile." It's such a fun happy song that makes you feel good. Keep smiling and letting that amazing spirit of yours shine bright. You will be amazed how much a smile and kind words can make someone's day.

Each one of us is unique in our own way. Being happy is something you can and should embrace. Don't hold back, let your smile shine and your spirit run free!

Be Kind to Yourself

You are amazing just the way you are. Don't try to be someone everyone else wants you to be. The person you see in the mirror is awesome! Its super important to take care of yourself, inside and out.

Remember to be kind to yourself and embrace your own beauty every day. Keep it simple and be YOU. Be a good person, give your best and love life.

Find Your Peace

Finding peace or being peaceful is so important at any age. Today is a good day to find your peace. What makes your mind rest and your heart sing? You owe it to yourself to have a peaceful day, filled with positive possibilities.

Even through tough times, allow your mind to be at ease. Understand that troubles don't last forever. Finding peace regularly keeps negative thoughts or energy to take over your mindset. Surround yourself with inspiring people and positive things.

POSITIVE THOUGHTS, POSITIVE VIBES!

Home Is Where the Heart Is

It's said, "home is where the heart is." My oldest son, Carter, will ask, "Daddy, what are we doing today?" I answer, "Not sure, what would you like to do?" He replies, "Stay home."

There is a comfort in being in the space you call home. It is a place where you feel love, safe and at peace. That's why your room is a special place in your home, because it's yours.

You can create a space that makes you feel good. Allow your home to be another space in your life that offers peace, love and positive energy.

Family Through the Generations

The bond you have with your family is something that will stay with you your whole life. Family loves you, supports you and helps you grow. Look back at your family tree and embrace the connection from the past into the present. You are a key part of for family's future.

We learn so much from family including love, understanding and respect, all while also building traditions. Together we form an amazing connection that extends through generations.

POSITIVE THOUGHTS, POSITIVE VIBES!

Power of Dreams

When your parents look into your eyes they see your potential. Take a look in the mirror; what do you see?

Bit by bit, piece by piece, you will continue to shape the person in the mirror. Looking into the mirror gives you a chance to reflect within. Believe in the power of your dreams and stay determined to succeed. Love who you are because we all have something positive to share.

POSITIVE THOUGHTS, POSITIVE VIBES!

Keep on Dreaming

Who said that your dreams are not possible?

We don't know the future, but if we stay focused it will unfold itself. Grab what you know and start with that. The road will get hard and you might not know where to turn. Trust yourself and if you get lost, pick up the pieces and reclaim what is yours.

Most successful people have stumbled a few times. So, stand tall and don't allow anything or anyone to knock you down.

Dreamers, keep on dreaming.

POSITIVE THOUGHTS, POSITIVE VIBES!

Healthy Living

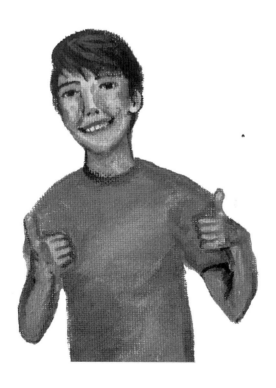

Eat Healthy

Stop eating all that candy. We know how much you love candy but moderation is important. Let that candy, ice cream, cookies or cake be a special treat. Over indulging on sweets can cause health problems that you do not want.

Take care of your body by eating a balanced diet and enjoying your favorite sweets from time to time.

POSITIVE THOUGHTS, POSITIVE VIBES!

Eat Super Fuels

Don't want to eat those veggies and fruits, do you? Today and every day you should choose to fuel your amazing body with foods that are not only delicious but also give you strength.

My good friend and Health Coach Jacki Dalismer is passionate about helping people be the best version of themselves. She often talks about eating well and moving your body. Doing those things will give you the energy you need to tackle your day!

Fresh fruits, veggies and lean proteins are like your super fuel, helping you grow stronger and smarter every single day. We want you to be the happiest and the healthiest version of yourself.

Move Your Body

Being active is so important! I encourage my boys to get those bodies moving! Whether it's taekwondo, exercise or any type of sports related activities, moving your body is important. Would you like to sleep better? Move your body! Would you like to play better? Move your body!

Moving your body plays a major part in energizing your mind, body and soul. There are lots of options and it's OK to pick something that works for you. Listen to your parents when they say stop watching TV and go outside, LOL! We want you to grow up strong, healthy, and happy.

16

Finding Balance

You are a fantastic kid with amazing potential. Enjoying video games is great fun, but remember to also find balance in other activities that simulate your mind and body.

You can hear your parents telling you to take a break from the video games. I know it's another way to connect with friends but it's just as important to take breaks and be active with friends too. Manage your time wisely and create some balance with gaming.

Having a wide range of experiences is the key to healthy living.

POSITIVE THOUGHTS, POSITIVE VIBES!

Embrace the Music

Music has the power to turn any situation into a positive one. It inspires you, and fills your heart with joy. One song I love is, "Positive Vibration" by Bob Marley. Check it out.

I love all kinds of music, especially the tunes with a good beat. Let the melody guide you. Let the rhythm lift you. Allow the harmony to surround you.

It will allow you to express yourself in ways you could never imagine. Embrace the gift of music to create a positive vibration that will brighten up your day.

Stay In the Zone

It's all about having a positive outlook on life. You woke up this morning, the sun is shining and you got a good night's sleep. You're ready to soak in all the potential positive possibilities ahead of you in this day. Your positive energy is giving off an amazing vibe that the world needs. Hold your head up high and do your best to stay in the positive zone!

Trust In Yourself

It's okay to feel worried or anxious but always remember you are safe and loved. Take a few deep breaths! You can handle whatever comes your way.

It's normal to have ups and downs, but you will overcome challenges in your life. Talk about your feelings with someone you trust. Always remember it's okay to ask for help.

Knowing there are people who love you and want to help you can make a big difference. Trust in yourself and believe you have the tools to manage your anxiety.

Know Your Worth

Knowing your worth allows you to tap into the power you have inside to always be your best. Always remember to connect yourself and hang around people that make you feel good. Let me say it another way; "surround yourself with good people."

I mean people with good energy. The people that lift your spirits by just being around them. Know that you are worthy of love and respect no matter what. Let your light shine in the beautiful unique way only you can!

POSITIVE THOUGHTS, POSITIVE VIBES!

Good Decisions

You have the power to control your actions and choices. You might ask why it's important to make good choices. It's because your choices will impact your life now and in the future. Take a breath before you react to a situation.

Controlling your emotions and taking a step back to breathe could be what you need in a stressful moment. It takes practice but once you see the impact it has on you, you'll never go back.

POSITIVE THOUGHTS, POSITIVE VIBES!

Until You Blossom

You might often hear, "be patient." You are like a seed planted in the ground. Your parents guide your steps. That's the water you need and over time you're able to grow. Each day you're given the chance to grow, but it takes patience to see results.

Be a kid and enjoy all the wonderful things about being a kid. Soak in all the good with your eyes wide open and with an open heart.

Patience helps you stay positive while you wait for your dreams to blossom.

POSITIVE THOUGHTS, POSITIVE VIBES!

School is Cool

School Is Cool

Parents talk about it all the time. They keep talking about how important school is. I was so proud when my son Carter made the honor roll. It's cool to be smart! Yes, you might question... how can school be cool?

School is a place where you can learn new things every day, make friends, and discover your passions. It's where you grow into the amazing person you are meant to become! So yes, school is cool and so very important!

POSITIVE THOUGHTS, POSITIVE VIBES!

A Good Education

With a grumpy attitude you groan the question, "Why do I have to go to school this morning?" I know how hard it is to get out of bed some mornings. Remember, every day at school is a step towards building a bright future. School helps you grow and become the amazing adult we want to see. It's where you make friends, learn new things and tap into what your passions might be.

You might not understand it now but, getting a good education is the key to unlocking your dreams.

POSITIVE THOUGHTS, POSITIVE VIBES!

Responsibilities Make You Responsible

You may find yourself saying, "I don't understand why I have to do chores. Isn't doing my homework enough?"

Doing chores around the house and helping your parents with things helps you build important skills. Through that process, you're working on something called responsibility. Don't worry, you are capable of handling responsibilities and learning from them. Taking on tasks shows how mature and reliable you are becoming. Keep up the great work!

Your Powerful Mind

Benjamin Franklin said it best, "The doors of wisdom are never shut." You will keep growing and there is always something to learn. Keep your eyes open and your mind ready to learn.

I often say to my boys, "If someone is trying to teach you something, learn it. You never know what you're going to use in life."

Your mind is a powerful thing and will take you places you can only dream of.

POSITIVE THOUGHTS, POSITIVE VIBES!

Curiosity Can Lead to Greatness

Curiosity is a part of being a kid. You live in a big world with lots to learn and see. I get it. Each and every day you are trying to figure out how the world works. It's okay to ask questions. Each question you ask allows you to learn new things. It's all about the hows and whys in life.

Ask as many questions as you want. It is the best way to learn. Some of our great leaders used curiosity to do great things. You are next in line.

What Do You Want to Achieve?

We all have something that we really want to have or achieve. What is it that you want? It could be something small, and in the moment, or it could be something big you will work towards in our future.

Take a moment and write down what that is. Why is it so important to you? How would it make you feel, when and if you accomplish it? Then, go for it! Work towards achieving that goal.

Achievement is good for the soul.

Ask for Help

It's OK to ask for help. We all need someone at some point where we can ask "I need help." By asking for help you start the process of finding the solution. Surround yourself with good people who you feel comfortable with in your time of need. Asking for help can be the bravest thing you can do and something you will need to know how to do as an adult.

Teamwork Makes the Dream Work

During my son Harrison's Flag Football pre-game speech, we are always talking about teamwork. Teamwork is important because it allows us to achieve more than we could ever on our own.

There is a saying, "teamwork makes the dream work." When we work together and share our ideas, some amazing things can happen. Overall, working together makes the world a better place.

Patience Is a Virtue

You wrote down a goal you want to achieve. Now you might be asking how long it's going to take to accomplish. It takes hard work, time and patience. If you just realized how difficult it can be to wait, that's OK. Don't give up.

Sometimes good things come to those who wait. Patience is a virtue. Think of that as you move forward in achieving what you want and continue to move forward.

POSITIVE THOUGHTS, POSITIVE VIBES!

Don't Be Swayed by Peer Pressure

You hold the power to resist peer pressure. To say "No," to things you know are wrong. Your superpower within will say no. If you listen, you will be able to stand up for what is right.

Stand strong and be proud to be true to yourself. If you are second guessing something, don't be afraid to ask for help. Just because someone tells you to do it, or says it will be okay, you know in your heart what is right or wrong.

Trust yourself.

Controlling Your Reactions

Everyone around you is yelling and screaming! How do you stay clam when people are arguing? Remember that you cannot control how others act. You can only control how you react.

Try to focus on something peaceful, positive and remember tomorrow is another day. Take a few deep breaths, move to a quiet space and allow the situation to cool down. Be in control of your own feelings and use your superpower of positivity to get you through.

POSITIVE THOUGHTS, POSITIVE VIBES!

Put Minds Together

You don't have to do it all alone. While there are some things that only take one person to accomplish, most can be done with a team. Having people to partner with can make the task easier and even more fun.

The ability to understand and work with others is so important. Collectively we can have a huge impact on creating change in the world.

One person can light the spark, but it's up to the rest of us to keep the flame going.

Two minds are more powerful than one.

Stand Up for You

You are strong, kind, and deserve respect. When you treat others with kindness and stand up against bullying, you are making a difference. Believe in yourself and know that you are not defined by the words or actions of others.

Remember to always stand up for yourself and surround yourself with people who respect and appreciate you for being uniquely you. You are beautiful on the inside and out. Believe it, own it and share it.

POSITIVE THOUGHTS, POSITIVE VIBES!

Finish What You Start

Always finish what you start and say what you mean! If you have a project to do in school make sure to give your best and finish the project. If you tell your parents you're going to do something, make sure to do it.

Being true to yourself is key to becoming a responsible adult. We all have different techniques on how to accomplish things. It doesn't matter how it is done, but completing them is key!

POSITIVE THOUGHTS, POSITIVE VIBES!

Speak Up!

Communication with Positive Results

I get it, no one understands you. Trying to explain yourself to adults can be difficult sometimes. It's all about our crazy communication styles which can be a little different and tough to understand sometimes. Know your parents are always there for you even if you don't feel that way. Remember that they love you and want the best for you.

Keep those lines of communication open. It will lead you to positive results.

Open the Door to Communication

You have the potential to be a great communicator. Maybe, it's easy for you to connect with others, especially with your friends. Us parents will encourage, support and guide you along the way.

Face-to-face conversations with friends opens up the door to great communication possibilities. You're learning an important skill that will be powerful as you continue to get older.

POSITIVE THOUGHTS, POSITIVE VIBES!

Be Confident

Stand up strong and speak with confidence. Look someone in the eyes when you are speaking to them. That shows respect to the person and the conversation you're having. As you continue to get older, you will do the necessary things to fine tune the person that you're going to become.

Be confident in the things you have learned and your ability to keep learning. Your confidence grows every single day.

Keep soaking in all of the positivity that is around you.

Parents Just Don't Understand?

When I was your age, there was a song by DJ Jazzy Jeff and the Fresh Prince called, "Parents just don't understand." It's okay to feel like your parents don't understand you. It's a normal part of growing up. But at the end of the day remember, your parents love you and want the best for you.

Even though they don't always understand you, they still respect your feelings. As you get older you will be capable of making your own decisions and choices because of their guidance. Keep shining and enjoying your life right now.

Forgiveness is a Gift

Dr. Martin Luther King Jr said it best, "Darkness cannot drive out darkness; only light can do that. Hate cannot drive out hate; only love can do that."

Today, you choose to forgive and let go of any hurt or anger in your heart. Forgiveness is a gift you give to yourself. It frees you from negativity and brings peace to your mind.

Forgiveness is powerful, and it helps you grow stronger and happier each day.

POSITIVE THOUGHTS, POSITIVE VIBES!

Watch Your Confidence Grow

Can you feel how confident you are becoming? It's all about learning new experiences and trying new things. As your confidence grows it will allow you to achieve amazing things. We are all very excited to see what the future holds in right in front of you!

Take Time to Listen

You are the kind of person who seems to care about everyone else. Showing the ability to understand and share the feelings of others is called, empathy. When you care about how others feel, and try to understand what they are going through, you are being empathetic.

When you show kindness and understanding, you can make someone's day better. We all have the power to spread positivity by being empathetic. You can be a good friend, brother or sister when you take the time to listen. Taking the time to listen and understand others is a wonderful way to live.

Truth Sets You Free

I understand that you are very curious about stuff. A little bit of peer pressure from your friends encourages you to do something that you know in your heart is not right. When our parents question us about something it's important to always tell the truth. Because when you tell the truth your heart feels good and you understand things better.

There is an old saying "the truth will set you free," and it always will.

Emotional Well-Being

A Peaceful Feeling

What does peace feel like? Feeling peaceful is not allowing negative thoughts or energy to take over. Surround yourself with inspiring people and positive things. Put yourself in situations that offer a positive outcome. It's a good vibe that helps your mind to relax. You deserve to feel what peace feels like. Seek it out and then bask in it.

Allow a Laugh

They say laughing is the best medicine. Sometimes I laugh so hard that tears come out of my eyes. Laughing makes your soul feel good and sends positive energy to your mind and to others.

I love people who tell jokes and laugh at their own humor. The ability to allow yourself to laugh is one of the greatest gifts.

Look for those opportunities to let yourself go and take in the positive energy laughing can offer.

POSITIVE THOUGHTS, POSITIVE VIBES!

Believe in Yourself

It's so important to look in the mirror and love the person you see. From your nose, eyes, hair and skin color, you are unique and special. Lift yourself up and always remember to be kind to yourself. Let that positivity spread to those around you.

Embrace your strengths, and tap into your superpower, which is believing in yourself!

Stand Strong

Even when things get tough, hold your head up and stand strong. You will face moments that test your strength and willpower. These challenges can make you a stronger person and allow you to learn some valuable lessons.

Our growth and our ability to move forward comes through challenges That's what makes us who we are. Look for the silver lining and allow a little light in to help get you through it.

Believe in yourself and your ability to overcome anything that comes your way.

POSITIVE THOUGHTS, POSITIVE VIBES!

Love Conquers Hate

In this crazy world we live in, sometimes we forget that love conquers hate and unity eliminates division. We must be open to building bridges, instead of perpetuating hate, anger and ignorance.

Through love comes understanding and the ability to see past ourselves. We cannot let our egos cloud a pathway of being open minded.

You control what you feel for others. Can you see their beauty or just their flaws? Can you see beyond what might hurt and see what can heal?

Start with positivity and see what you get!

Gain Respect

Althea Franklin sang a song called "Respect." We gain respect by treating others with kindness and respect. It is also so important to respect ourselves. By showing respect, you create a positive and loving environment where everyone feels appreciated.

Us adults are here to teach you the importance of respect which will lead to strong healthy relationships.

POSITIVE THOUGHTS, POSITIVE VIBES!

Big Feelings

It's completely normal to have big emotions. You need to try to not let them control you. Remember, it's okay to feel this way and you can always talk about your feelings with someone you trust.

Take deep breaths, maybe count to 10, and know that you are loved and supported no matter what you are feeling. You are doing great!

It's Okay to Feel Angry

At some point, something is going to make you angry. It's okay to feel angry. Just like feeling happy or sad, anger is an emotion. When you feel angry, just take deep breaths or talk to someone you trust. With a positive outlook you can turn that anger into something positive.

Choose to voice your anger in a good way and find solutions to make things better. Today and every day you will stay in control of your emotions and give the situation your best positive energy.

You have the Power

Being brave and strong is not always easy. Facing your fears takes courage. Look deep down inside to find the strength to face what scares you and keep going. When things get tough, you can be brave and stand tall.

Keep believing in yourself and your abilities. Grow the courage to try new things, face challenges and overcome obstacles because you are very courageous. You have unlimited power to be the best person you can be.

POSITIVE THOUGHTS, POSITIVE VIBES!

Respect Yourself

How do you respect and love yourself?

When we respect ourselves, we show others how we would like to be treated. When we love ourselves, our true selves will shine bright for the world to see.

It is up to us to understand that we're not here to be accepted by everyone. Look within yourself and love and respect who you are.

POSITIVE THOUGHTS, POSITIVE VIBES!

The Power to Create Your Own Happiness

Everyone wants to be happy, right? You have the power to create your own happiness. Look for the good in every day, and every situation. Focus on what you can control and let go of what you cannot. Your attitude and mindset shape your reality, so choose to see the bright side of things.

Embrace each day with a smile and an open heart. Know that you have the strength to overcome any challenges that come your way. Stay positive and see the good even in those difficult situations. You hold the key to your happiness!

Stay True to Yourself

It's said that honesty is the best policy. It's not always easy to do the right thing, especially when no one is watching. But being honest means you are being true to yourself.

Staying true to yourself is a super important way to be. Give from your heart, and allow your soul to feel free. Your honesty will shine bright and help guide you to make the best choices.

POSITIVE THOUGHTS, POSITIVE VIBES!

Acts of Kindness

Today is your day to be kind. A single act of kindness can have a positive rippling effect. Share of yourself and the next person may share with someone else.

When we give to others it makes our heart feel good. Being kind frees your spirit and pushes away the negativity.

Express Yourself

It's completely okay to feel upset sometimes. There are so many emotions running through your body. It's OK to acknowledge them. Find the best way to express yourself and seek support from trusted adults or friends when you're feeling upset. You are never alone in dealing with your emotions. Allow the positive energy from within to help you through the process.

Playtime is Essential

Take a Break

Sometimes you just need a break. School, friends and all the things going on in life can be a bit much. Take a moment to stop, breathe and allow your spirit to rest. No one is expecting you to be on your A game all the time. It's important to communicate with your loved ones when things feel like they are becoming a bit too much. Keep shining brightly. It's OK to take a break!

Create Memories Outside

My son, Harrison, says it's super fun to play outside because you can do tons of fun stuff. Things like play on the trampoline, ride your bike and laugh with friends.

You can explore nature, feel the sunshine on your face, and have some amazing time with friends. Go outside and let nature create some awesome memories.

You will be glad you did.

POSITIVE THOUGHTS, POSITIVE VIBES!

Play Outside

Do you like playing outside? Whether it's riding scooters, or swinging on a swing, take some time to enjoy the peacefulness of the outdoors. Playing outside allows you to explore new things, gaining different perspectives. Time seems to fly by and your heart feels good.

Seeds of Possibility

We all love dreaming about the future. Plant seeds of possibility in your heart and watch them grow. It's exciting to think about all the amazing things you could do and become. I get it, you don't have all the answers right now. It's OK.

Life is a big adventure, and part of the fun is figuring things out as you go along. So, keep dreaming and exploring what's next. It is full of endless possibilities.

POSITIVE THOUGHTS, POSITIVE VIBES!

Smell the Roses

There's a saying, "Take some time to smell the roses." It means, take a moment and enjoy the beauty that is all around you. Take a moment to enjoy the flowers, birds, the sunset, and a full moon. So many little things around you that can add some positivity to your day.

Recognizing and soaking up all the positive things around you is so awesome. The beauty and positivity surrounding you are there to be embraced; so, cherish your ability to appreciate them.

Cherish Moments

I think about the many memories and traditions that I'm creating with my boys. Everything from a special yearly event with family, or running a race for charity.

You too can create special memories with family and friends. These will add up to be something really special that you can share with others. The happy times will be imprinted on your mind forever. So always cherish the moments you spend with your family and friends, creating those magical moments.

Let Your Spirit Be Free

There is nothing like connecting with friends. You can do that by going to the playground and running around while you talk about fun stuff. Being able to play and be free is so important when it comes to being a kid. The goal is simple. Have fun! Soak up the sun, feel the breeze and let your spirit be free!

Life's Simplest Pleasures

My son, Harrison, loves the opportunity to be in the water, and if not in it, near it. The splash of water when a turtle leaps in from a log. The plop of the bait as he throws out his line hoping to catch a fish.

There is a peacefulness about fishing that allows you to connect with nature. Nature allows you to just be, and enjoy what life has to offer. Harrison finds joy in knowing and remembering that life's simplest pleasures are often easy to find.

Know Your Friends

Take some time to thank your true friends. Through the good and bad times, your true friends are there.

Through growth, you can distinguish between those who are true friends and those who are not. A best friend has lived the stories with you and will walk with you through fire.

They touch your heart because they look deep into your soul. Know who your true friends are and it will help you figure out the ones who are not.

POSITIVE THOUGHTS, POSITIVE VIBES!

Balance Social Media

Remember, it's important to balance your time on social media with other activities that you enjoy. Those devices will find a way to keep you engaged! You are in control of how you use your time. It might not be easy but take breaks, participate in healthy activities, and spend quality time offline.

A More Social You

You have some of the best friends in the whole wide world. We have so many things in common through this amazing thing called friendship. Hip Hop group Whodini had a song when I was your age called "Friends." A quote from that song is, "Some you grew up with from around the way and you're still real close to this very day."

Be grateful for your long-term and short-term friendships. They will come in all shapes, sizes and colors. Having amazing friends is helping you to become more social and become a well-rounded person.

Balance Your Time

I watch my boys get all caught up in this crazy thing called YouTube shorts. LOL.

Funny quick segments that you have to continue to scroll through, while struggling to turn them off. These keep you engaged with video after video.

I get it, we all enjoy a good laugh, but it's always super important to balance our TV time with reading, outdoors, play time, etc.

POSITIVE THOUGHTS, POSITIVE VIBES!

Some Face Time

We are living in a society where technology has taken over. The word "conversation" takes on a different form. Texting, emailing, social media messaging are ways we communicate now. But nothing feels better than face-to-face time with your friends.

Being able to hear and see someone's expression really makes the difference. Enjoy the opportunity for a little face to face time every chance you get.

POSITIVE THOUGHTS, POSITIVE VIBES!

Working Towards Your Future

Change Is Not Easy

Change helps you grow and learn new things. It's okay to feel a little scared sometimes. Surround yourself with people who inspire your spirit and offer help in your time of need.

Change can be difficult because learning new things takes patience. How hard are you willing to work? How bad do you want to do your best, and be your best?

Change is a part of life so look around and ask your folks for help. The process is not always easy but people are willing to help you.

POSITIVE THOUGHTS, POSITIVE VIBES!

No Stopping You

Back in the 80's a hit movie came out called, "Breakin." My boys might remember us watching it over and over on DVD. One of my favorite songs from that movie is "There's no stopping us!" Life will be filled with detours, pot holes and wrong turns but there is no stopping you.

You are strong, capable and have the ability to get through the tough times. Lean on the amazing people around and continue to keep moving forward. Listen to the song in your heart and keep your feet moving to the beat.

Give Back

Every year through the PMJ Foundation we do a holiday and back-to-school drive. My two sons Carter and Harrison have been participating since they were born. I am grateful for the opportunity to teach my children the importance of giving back. I know that by doing so, I am helping them to become more compassionate and responsible adults.

The Power of Positivity

One look at you and others will see the power of positivity through your eyes. Keep being curious and wondering what this world is all about. Find joy in the simplest things and approach challenges with a positive attitude. Someone is watching, listening and taking in your light. Allow it to shine and never underestimate your possibilities of making a positive impact.

What Is Trust?

You might often hear people use the word trust. Sometimes it's difficult to understand what trust truly is. Every day, adults trust you to make good choices and learn from your experiences. Just like every day you trust you'll have dinner on the table.

Keep trusting others who care for and support you. Know that you are capable of facing any challenge that will come your way.

POSITIVE THOUGHTS, POSITIVE VIBES!

Live With Purpose

One of my favorite artists, Jonathan McReynolds sings a song that has the lyrics, "I'm not lucky. I'm loved." Know that your best self is the person you are.

From your hair, eyes and the clothes you wear. Your uniqueness is just beautiful. The world is a better place having you in it.

Walk, talk and live with purpose for the importance of you is valuable to the world.

POSITIVE THOUGHTS, POSITIVE VIBES!

You are the Painter

Living within our universe and painting the picture we show the world, we create a canvas filled with different colors blending into one story. That's your story!

We all have a picture to paint, a gift to the world. You are the painter of your story and it needs to be shared. Someone, somewhere will see, hear and feel who and what you are.

Your Share of Challenges

You should be very proud of the person you are today and the person you are becoming.

You will face your share of challenges and situations in life where you feel a little lost. But many of those situations will be life learning experiences that will allow you to continue to grow and learn and move forward. Along the way you will find the things that you are very, very good at.

POSITIVE THOUGHTS, POSITIVE VIBES!

Attracting Positive Energy

How do we attract positive energy? Learn to see the positive in any situation. It's not possible to be in control of every situation. Whether it's school, friends, parents etc. try to see the positive but not looking for the negative.

We all have the ability to allow positive energy within. I mean seriously, who really wants to live in negativity? Put yourself in positive situations, around positive people, so you can attract that positive energy.

POSITIVE THOUGHTS, POSITIVE VIBES!

See the Positive

Learn to see the positive in any situation. We all have the ability to allow positive energy within. I mean seriously, who really wants to live in negativity? Put yourself in positive situations, around positive people, think positively and let your light shine.

Respect Yourself

New people will come into your life all of the time. When we respect ourselves, we show them how we would like to be treated. When we love ourselves, our true selves will shine bright for the world to see.

Your goal is not to focus on being accepted by everyone, but simply loving yourself.

Love and respect who that person is and look within.

Create the Change

With this book, you have the opportunity to join the Positive Vibes movement. The mission is to create the change you want to see in the world around you. There are so many different ways to show someone Positive Vibes.

You can show it through your kindness, support and of course your smile. You can be a positive force for good and to make a difference in the lives of others.

When you help to find the good, you help to spread positive vibes to others.

Make A Change

Michael Jackson said it best, "If you want to make the world a better place, take a look at yourself and make a change."

We all have the ability to create change whether big or small. Let's not look to our right or left but in front of the mirror and allow that person to create change.

Be the creator of the change you seek.

Face Your Fears

How do you stare fear in the face? You have to look deep within and use your past experience to provide strength.

It's not easy to do, or attempt something you fear. Taking the leap will not be easy but the outcome could be worth it.

You will never know what you can do unless you try. Through this process you will find out more about yourself. Build confidence in the old and new you.

POSITIVE THOUGHTS, POSITIVE VIBES!

Keep Your Promises

When you promise to do something, like clean your room, you should keep that promise. But it is also important to not make promises you can't keep. Sometimes we make promises that are tough to keep or that you know you shouldn't keep.

Stay true to yourself and focus on just giving your best. Don't stress about making everyone happy, be real with yourself first, and don't make promises if you don't mean it. Superheroes are not needed all the time. The only promise you truly need to keep is taking care of yourself.

About the Author

Preston Mitchum Jr. has dedicated his life to giving back and making a difference. Born in Bronx, New York his family moved to Langley Park, MD in 1981.

His family established the Mitchum Lawn and Landscaping business shortly after. Preston's father, Mitchum Sr. worked here for over 30 years, creating beautiful lawns and establishing relationships throughout the community.

Preston Jr. is a graduate of Towson State University where he took his love for video and became an 18-year veteran news photographer for WMAR-TV in Baltimore, Maryland.

During this time, he founded The PMJ Foundation to create change in the Baltimore community. The foundation's vision is to impact families through programs and services that offer positive growth. The foundation has served thousands throughout Maryland.

With the passing of his father, Preston has taken over the family business and will continue to provide the quality service that his family established for many years.

Other Books

 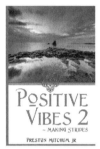 

A portion of the proceeds of this book will support the programs that the PMJ Foundation offers. Preston hopes that the positive message this book has to offer will impact thousands and create positive vibes that we all can feel.

The PMJ Foundation

*PRESENTING POSSIBILITIES
FOR BRIGHTER FUTURES*

The PMJ Foundation's Career Awareness Project (CAP) after-school program brings the outside professional world into the classroom. Community volunteers present their careers to our participants which engage our at-risk youth to explore the infinite possibilities of college and career choices that are available.

~

To learn more about the PMJ Foundation please visit: **www.pmjfoundation.org**

About the Illustrator

Baltimore based artist, **Melissa Le Roux**, has been honing her creative skills for the last several years. A self-proclaimed animal enthusiast, nature lover, adventure seeker, and a travel explorer. Her passion for the acrylic arts was ignited in 2021 and has been fueled by travel. From her travel adventures she has created a series of paintings. Her series of travel paintings includes landscapes, animals, and people. Her commissioned work includes animals and people. She is passionate about helping others, regularly volunteers, and has made art donations. Overall, she enjoys art, has a creative eye, and is a mother who is loving the adventure of raising her two beautiful girls. Live by the moment, but learn from your past.

References

Shanice "I Love your Smile" from the 1991 Album *Inner Child*

Bob Marley & the Wailers "Positive Vibration" from the 1976 Album *Bob Marley & the Wailers*

DJ Jazzy Jeff and the Fresh Prince "Parents Just Don't Understand" from the 1988 Album *He's the DJ, I'm the Rapper*

Aretha Franklin "Respect" from the 1967 Album *I Never Loved a Man the Way I Love You*

Whodini "Friends" from the 1984 Album *Escape*

Song from the Movie *Breakin* "There's No Stopping Us" by Ollie & Jerry 1984

Lyrics by Jonathan McReynolds from the song "Not Lucky, I'm loved" from the 2018 Album *Make Room*

ERIN GO BRAGH
Publishing

Erin Go Bragh Publishing publishes various genres of books for numerous authors. Their portfolio consists of a 1200-page Vietnamese to English Dictionary, Historical fiction, an award-winning children's educational series, multiple adult novels and memoirs, tween adventure stories, as well as Christian Fiction. Their objective is to promote literacy and education through reading and writing.

www.ErinGoBraghPublishing.com
Canyon Lake, Texas

Made in the USA
Middletown, DE
07 March 2025

72304872R10059